THE PUBLISHED PASTOR

Expanding Your Ministry through Writing and Publishing

I0116124

Dr. Tim Riordan

THE PUBLISHED PASTOR

Expanding Your Ministry through Writing and Publishing

Dr. Tim Riordan

GreenTree Publishers
Newnan, Georgia

The Published Pastor –

Expanding Your Ministry through Writing
Copyright © 2015 by Timothy E. Riordan

Unless otherwise noted, Scripture is taken from the NEW AMERICAN STANDARD BIBLE®, Copyright © 1960,1962, 1963,1968,1971,1972, 1973,1975,1977,1995 by The Lockman Foundation. Used by permission. (www.Lockman.org)

Scripture quotations marked (NIV) are taken from the Holy Bible, New International Version®, NIV®. Copyright © 1973, 1978, 1984, 2011 by Biblica, Inc.™ Used by permission of Zondervan. All rights reserved worldwide. www.zondervan.com The "NIV" and "New International Version" are trademarks registered in the United States Patent and Trademark Office by Biblica, Inc.™

Printed in the United States of America

ISBN-13: 978-1-944483-08-1 (GreenTree Publishers)
ISBN-10: 1-944483-08-X

Follow Dr. Tim Riordan through the following media links:
Website/blog: www.timriordan.me
Twitter: @tim_riordan
Facebook: www.facebook.com/pages/Tim-Riordan/ 453213784820641

Greentree Publishers
www.greentreepublishers.com

CONTENTS

Chapter One - Climbing Mount Everest.........................1

Chapter Two - Who Me? A Writer?................................7

Chapter Three - Multiple Points of Impact 15

Chapter Four - Half the Work is Done.........................23

Chapter Five - Narrowing Your Topic..........................37

Chapter Six - Preparing to Write Your Book 45

Final Thoughts 57

Note from the Author...61

Personal Contact Page..62

More Books from Greentree Publishers 63

Notes...67

DEDICATION

This book is dedicated to my wonderful team who labors tirelessly to take my work and make it presentable. A writer stands tall when he stands on other people's shoulders.

Special Thanks...

No one is a self-made man (or woman). Success always comes as a result of a wonderful community working together. I am so blessed to be a part of the SonRise Church family in Newnan, Georgia and to have a host of other friends who have helped to make this book a reality.

I was able to complete this writing project because of the sacrifices of many people like my assistant, June Black, and another SonRise staff member: Judy Miller. I would also like to thank the SonRise Writers' group for their support and editorial help and a host of other people who read my manuscript before publication. I am also grateful to my editor, Adele Brinkley, and my wonderful family.

CHAPTER ONE

Climbing Mount Everest

You might be a preacher if...

- you've ever dreamed you were preaching only to awaken and discover that you were;
- you see a picnic as no picnic;
- you've been tempted to take up an offering at a family reunion;
- you show up for Sunday lunch with your lapel microphone still in place;
- your sermons have a happy ending...everyone is happy when they end;
- you've ever wanted to give the soundman some feedback of your own.

Here's one more that is the basis for this book: you might be a preacher if you have tons of life-changing material in your files, but you have never extended your ministry by writing a book.

God has called us as conduits through whom He works to grow people to be more like Jesus. We spend many of our waking hours trying to be used by God to accomplish that Kingdom purpose.

What if I could show you a way to multiply your ministry effectiveness so that your teaching/preaching ministry has greater impact? Would you do it?

Writing and publishing books can bear more fruit through your ministry than you have ever imagined. Just consider the impact pastors like Rick Warren and Max Lucado have had on the world because of their writing ministries. You may think that you can never be like one of these well-known pastors, but I know firsthand that you can reach around the world through your books.

Because you are reading this book, I assume that you have at least some interest in being a published writer. It is possible you have just been unable to get started. It may seem a little like considering a climb up Mt. Everest: it would be fun and rewarding, but it really seems like an impossible feat. Writing a book is not impossible, and it could greatly impact your ministry on a daily basis.

Who Will Benefit From This Book?

This book is the first of a series of three books entitled *The Published Pastor*. The purpose of this series is two-fold:

- I want to encourage you to become a writer.
- I will give you the tools needed to write and publish your books.

I used the word *Pastor* in the title of this series, and I know this position applies to a variety of people with varying ministry responsibilities. Whether you are a senior pastor or a leader in children's ministry, these books offer helpful guidance as you consider writing and publishing. Are you a lay leader who teaches on a regular basis? These principles will also apply to your ministry.

You may have previously written books, and you are interested in how to improve your writing and publishing ministry. This series can be an important tool offering fresh ideas and new resources that will make your next book the best one yet. If you are not overwhelmed by the prospects of writing, the second book in this series may be more beneficial to you than the first. However, I do encourage you to read this first book as well because one particular nugget in it may be golden for you.

You may have never written a book but always wanted to pen one. This series will offer you a step-by-step plan that will ultimately end with a completed book. If you have no doubt that you can write, it is possible you simply need a kick-start. As the ancient Greek philosopher Epictetus said, "If you want to be a writer, write." Fast forwarding to the 21st Century, follow Nike's slogan–*Just Do It*.

Some of the encouragements I offer may not be needed in order for you to become a successful writer. However, my prayer is that you will find God using them to urge you on to complete your writing project. As He told Jeremiah, *Thus says the Lord, the God of Israel, "Write all the words which I have spoken to you in a book"* (Jeremiah 30:2).

Do you tremble at the thoughts of writing and believe you can never be a published author? This book is for you. We tend to elevate authors to a superhero status and look up to them as being people who seem to be more than just mere mortals. I offer a plan that will make writing and publishing your first book a real probability. I do not want to mislead you into thinking that writing is a simple task, however. It is far from simple, and you will find that it can be downright challenging.

Although writing a book may prove to be quite demanding, the results are well worth the effort. *You can do all things through Christ who strengthens you*, and God is simply looking for someone who is willing to be used. I believe that within the next year or so, your book can be a tool God uses to make a difference in the world.

The Time is Now

Never before has a greater need existed to write God's answer for our desperate world. We must look for ways to multiply ourselves and impact our world. Writing and publishing books can be one of our ministry tools tucked away in our toolbox that God will use to change lives.

I encourage you to read through all three books of this series prayerfully and with an open mind to what God may want to do through you. Work through the action points and find someone to hold you accountable to the commitments you make along the way. Make a commitment now that by this time next year, you will be a published author – or at least well on your way to accomplishing that goal.

The words to the prophet Habakkuk were specific to him as a prophet to Israel, but they remind Christian writers of the challenge before us today: *Then the LORD said to me, "Write my answer plainly on tablets, so that a runner can carry the correct message to others."* (Habakkuk 2:2, NLT)

Action Points

- Take a few moments to imagine how writing a book will expand your ministry. Write down at least three positive results you will experience by publishing a book.

- What are some of the barriers that you think may hinder you from writing and publishing a book? Write them down.

- I described at least three types of readers: those who have already published a book, those who have not published but are confident of success, and those who tremble at the thoughts of writing a book. Which of these types best describes you and why?

- Are you willing to take proactive steps now so that in a year or so, you will be a published author? Why not take a moment before reading any further to pray about what God would like to teach you through reading this book? Ask Him to open up your mind and your heart to His promptings.

- Do you have a prayer partner? If not, why not enlist one to pray with you about expanding your ministry through writing? Make a list of a few requests you would like to share with your prayer partner as you look into the possibility of becoming a published author.

CHAPTER TWO

Who Me? A Writer?

When I was in high school, I did not like English class. The thought of diagraming sentences nearly gave me the hives, and the idea of writing a paper would probably have sent me to the trauma center. Even now, my spelling is atrocious (thanks to spell check, I spelled that word correctly).

I could create a long list explaining why I cannot be a writer, but I think Paul's words in Colossians challenges us to do everything possible to make Christ known:

> *We proclaim Him, admonishing every man and teaching every man with all wisdom, so that we may present every man complete in Christ. For this purpose also I labor, striving according to His power, which mightily works within me.* (Colossians 1:28-29)

Our writing may come about from an act of "labor" through great "striving," but it is always God's power that bears fruit through our ministries.

I have a presupposition that I really believe to be true: If you can write a sermon, you can write a book.

Although every pastor writes sermons differently and every teacher develops unique lessons, each can write sermons or lessons that can become useful publications. In the following chapters, I will share with you important principles to transform your weekly sermon or Bible study into a chapter of your next book.

Once you decide to write, think of yourself as a writer. When I mentally began to see myself as a writer, this perspective affected my actions significantly. As a writer, I must be a reader, and I must have a system for formulating my research. I must be disciplined to have a time and a place to write every day. I must seek critique from other writers, and I must write and share my work with others in order to influence their lives.

Overcoming the Obstacles

Even if you are not a writer now, you can become one. Knowing the rules of English grammar is a plus, and being a handy wordsmith is helpful, but a number of tools are available to help you conquer any literary obstacle. Your greatest obstacle may be your own lack of confidence.

Moses tried to get out of leading the Exodus by pointing out to God his inadequacies. That rationale didn't work for Moses, and it won't work for us.

Keep in mind the words of Jesus in John 15:5: *I am the vine, you are the branches; he who abides in Me and I in him, he bears much fruit, for apart from Me you can do nothing.* While you are inadequate to do many things, God is more than adequate to do everything.

Another obstacle you must overcome is comparing yourself to other writers. It is easy to read Francis Chan, David Jeremiah, or A. W. Tozier and think you could never write like they do. The good news is you do not have to. God doesn't expect you to be Platt or Tozier. He only expects you to be you. The fact is your writing ministry will reach people that Tozier will never reach. People will read your book simply because they know you or have a relative who attends your church. Your book may be the only title they read in the next five years. You have a wonderful opportunity to provide Kingdom influence with people who otherwise may not be influenced spiritually.

One of my greatest obstacles was time. I later determined it was not a time issue but rather a priority and a discipline issue. I am a very busy person. I have a wonderful wife with six awesome children and one beautiful granddaughter. I pastor a growing church, and I have other responsibilities that also require my time.

I have wanted to write books since I was a young adult, but I managed to put it off until my forties. I kept telling myself that I did not have time to write. My problem was that I was trying to "eat the elephant" in one bite. I needed to apply the *one bite at a time* principle. You can only write a book one word at a time. The key to becoming a successful writer is to discipline yourself to write daily. I do not have the luxury of devoting large amounts of time to writing, but I try to write a little every day. Sometimes you may miss your writing appointment,

but if writing becomes a priority, you will have a published book before long.

Charles Swindoll was once asked how he could write
so many books. He replied that he simply wrote one
hour per day. This practice does not mean we should
avoid trying to carve out larger blocks of time for
writing, but it does mean we can be effective writers by
making a daily commitment to write.

My church gave me a two-week sabbatical last year,
and I spent a large part of it writing. I enjoyed this
opportunity immensely. I try to calendar in larger
pockets of time for writing, but most of my writing is
done in thirty minutes to one hour sessions.

"I do not know enough to write a book," you may
say. I have it on good authority that you do not have to
be an Einstein to be an author. You may even find that
methodical research and good systems of note taking
trumps stored up knowledge any day.

It is possible that the lack of knowledge obstacle
points to the fear of not knowing how to write or publish
a book. Well, that is why you are reading this book. A
number of good books are available that will help you
become a better writer. Writer's groups exist in many
cities, and online Christian writing conferences are held
often and in many locations. Even the process of
publishing books has become much more accessible to
the average person. I will address that topic in the second
book of this series.

For a long time, I felt like I could not be a successful
writer because I did not have a large platform. In other

words, I pastor a church of only few hundred instead of a few thousand. I am a nobody who wants somebody to read my books. It is true that a large platform is certainly a help, but it is not a requirement to be a successful writer. With the help of social media and networking, literally anyone could be the next best-selling author.

I have written more about your platform in the third book of this series because it is certainly important. Your success will be greater if you work strategically to enlarge your platform and follow specific, prescribed tasks on a regular basis. Even so, many authors start out as unknown writers who have a small platform and through God's grace become very influential authors.

"I can't afford to publish a book." I have said that one before, and it was really true back then. In the past, you had to spend a few thousand dollars to self-publish your book. Those days are gone. While it is really best to spend a little money on editing and cover design, you can actually write and publish a book at no cost. I'll show you how in the second book of the series.

One final obstacle I had to overcome was my inability to get a publisher. My first book was actually a novel I simply wrote for fun and then decided to try to publish. I sent out query letters to publishers and agents and could probably wallpaper my bedroom with the rejection letters I received. I finally published that book myself under a pen name to help raise money for one of my daughters to go on a mission trip.

That first book began my self-publishing journey that has taught me many wonderful skills and ideas that hopefully I can pass along to you. Because of this initial project, I started my own publishing company and have helped others publish their books.

Crossing the Line

Regardless of the obstacles to writing, you can overcome them. It does take determination and discipline. Once you cross the line and make the decision to be a writer, don't look back. Ecclesiastes 9:10 says, *Whatever your hand finds to do, do it with all your might.* Satan will give you fifty reasons why you should not write, but we know that he is not the one calling the shots in your life.

I can tell you one thing that will help you to be a better writer is a friend. I receive great encouragement from a circle of friends that include my wife, assistant, fellow staff members, family members, church members, and members of writers' groups. You need people in your life who will both encourage you and speak truth to you. If your writing is really bad, you need someone who loves you enough to tell you that it is bad. That does not mean you shouldn't write, but it does mean you need to work harder. Consider all criticism; it's better to make multiple revisions than to submit a faulty manuscript for publication.

I mentioned the idea of writers' groups. I am a member of a few writers' groups online. I also started a Christian writers' group in my community, which meets once a month at my church. In addition to that, I established a Facebook group (called *The Writing Pastor/*

Teacher) specifically for pastors and teachers who feel called to write. I invite you to find the page and join.

We all need encouragement, prayer, support, marketing help, fresh ideas, someone to read our first chapter, book reviews, etcetera. These groups offer this kind of support. I encourage you to participate in a local group.

Counting the Cost

If you are going to be a published author, you must not be only a writer. You must also be a rewriter. James Michener once said, "I have never thought of myself as a good writer. Anyone who wants reassurance of that should read one of my first drafts. But I am one of the world's great rewriters."

Your first draft is NEVER the finished product. I spent two years writing *Immovable: Standing Firm in the Last Days*, and then I spent another year rewriting it before it was ready for publication. If you are going to be a successful writer, you need to learn the art of rewriting.

I do think you must pray about the prospects of becoming a writer. You should count the costs of adding this extension of your ministry to your already busy schedule. Writing is hard work, and it takes time and commitment. However, I believe writing is a wonderful way to multiply your effectiveness as a spiritual leader and offers residual benefits as it continues to bear fruit.

As you pray about becoming an author, I believe you will discern whether or not God is calling you to write.

Writing may be an overflow of your general call to ministry or you may feel specifically called to be an author; nevertheless, you write in response to fulfilling your ministry in the world.

At times, I continue to serve in ministry because I am called; that may be the only reason I have moved forward at certain points in my life. You will experience times when writing is more hard work than fun, and the thing that might keep you on track to finish your manuscript is that sense of calling.

Action Points

- I said earlier that I struggled with English in high school. What challenges in your life could be seen as hindrances to becoming a successful writer?
- Do you see yourself as a writer? What difference would seeing yourself as a writer make?
- What is your reaction to the statement, "If you can write a sermon, you can write a book"?
- Review the seven obstacles to being a successful writer. Do you struggle with any of these obstacles? What steps will you take to overcome this struggle?
- I underscored the importance of being a part of a writer's group. Are you a member of one yet? Would you be willing to join my Facebook group *The Writing Pastor/Teacher* or another writer's group?
- Will you make a commitment to be a writer? Have you considered the cost and are you ready to take the plunge?

CHAPTER THREE

Multiple Points of Impact

Two of the pastors who work with me are avid fishermen. On a recent staff retreat, one of them took his boat, and we spent some of our breaks out on the lake cruising, relaxing, and talking.

I am fairly ignorant when it comes to fishing, so it was fascinating to hear about some of the finer points of the sport. Actually, there is a lot more to the sport than I first realized. I noticed immediately that this pastor had more than one fishing pole in the boat. It seems that when he fishes in a tournament, he places different types of bait on different poles. If the fish are not biting one type of bait, he casts another hook with different bait into the water.

God has called us to the ministry of fishing…for people, that is. For Christians, and specifically pastors, we have numerous *hooks* to use for our ministries' effectiveness. One hook is certainly preaching, while another is pastoral care. We could probably generate a list of hooks that help us bear fruit for the Kingdom. One of those could be writing.

Using Various Writing Methods

Even within the context of writing, hooks may vary. Let's go back to the fishing illustration. Though I am about to reveal nearly everything I know about fishing, my information is true. Not only do you use various types of bait for different fish or even for the same fish but at different times, you also use assorted hooks. The size and shape of the hook and the type of lure that is connected to it affect whether or not you have fish for dinner.

I favor non-fiction books about theological issues or practical ministry instruction, so I enjoy writing non-fiction books that encourage people in their spiritual lives. I know that I reach a certain kind of person with the non-fiction, Bible-teaching hook.

I discovered quite by accident that I reach a totally different audience with fiction. This reality should have been obvious, but sometimes I am a little slow. If you would have told me fifteen years ago that I had novel writing in my future, I would have laughed at the notion. It turns out that my first, official book was a novel.

Once my novel became available on Amazon, I really thought I would never write another work of fiction in my life. I saw it as a waste of my time. I also felt a little guilty for indulging myself in this genre because I felt like there were more important non-fiction books that I should have been writing.

I must confess that writing fiction is a lot of fun. I find myself experiencing aspects of the story as if I were present, so novel writing for me is a great mental vacation. In order to write about scuba diving in the Bahamas, I had to be the third diver observing the events that happened underwater.

Because those who read my novel have wondered about a sequel, I began to think about this hook of fiction in a different light. Fiction writing is a great way to insert spiritual principles and teach biblical truths. John Bunyan must have agreed, or he never would have written *Pilgrim's Progress*.

I did not think I was skilled enough to write a novel, but I simply set my mind to do it and gave it my best effort. I had to study about writing fiction, and I listened to novels (I downloaded mp3's from the library) to study how the authors communicated their story lines. If I "read" (listen to) fiction, I prefer to do it when I am driving or exercising. I have learned a lot through the process, so my sequel is much improved. After writing the sequel, I went back and rewrote the first book and made it into two different novels.

Since I added novel writing to my resume, I have noticed ways fiction could have a spiritual influence on the world. The first chapter of my book on Psalms tells the fictional story of how a family living in En Gedi in 800 B.C. used the Psalms in daily living. I will soon start my sequel to *Immovable* called *Immovable Kids*—a non-fiction book on how to prepare our children to stand firm during times of great spiritual warfare. I plan to write a companion novel to coincide with my non-fiction book on parenting for the last days. The novel will depict a family who implements the principles of my non-fiction book.

If I had never decided to "play around" with writing a fictional story, which ended up being my first novel, I never would have discovered this additional hook that has expanded my ministry influence. Here's the lesson I learned that I would like to pass along to you: do not cut yourself short. My mother used to tell me that I could do anything I wanted to do if I wanted to do it badly enough. I am not saying you *should* write fiction, but I am saying you *could* write fiction. Be open to how God may want to lead you to use various hooks in order to reach people with His life-changing message.

Fiction and non-fiction are not really the only options. Several different categories exist within these two broad genres. You could write Bible studies, devotionals, how-to books, or personal interest stories. You could write humor, allegory, or an autobiography. I know people who specialize in writing other people's stories.

Regardless of the hooks you employ, God can use them to accomplish His purpose. He is simply looking for someone who is willing to be used.

Advantages to a Writing Ministry

Consider these advantages to using writing as a tool to multiply your ministry effectiveness:

- It provides an additional resource for sermon impact. Most people will only remember ten percent, or less, of your sermon from a typical

Sunday message. If you write a book on the same topic, your congregation has a much greater opportunity to remember more than ten percent. They can read the chapter connected to a particular sermon and hopefully retain much more of your message. Your church members not only may retain it because of reading your book, but they also have a resource for additional study. Your book can also guide them in personal application in ways your sermon may not be able to address.

- If you have a congregation of 100, 200, or more attenders, your ministry may be multiplied two or three times as your congregation purchases your books and gives them away to others.

- You can have a gift for guests who visit your church.

- Your book can be a resource for discussion in your church small groups or Sunday School.

- Your book can be used by your congregation as an outreach tool in the community.

- You will be recognized as a published author and may have additional opportunities to speak.

- Through social media and online resources, people from all over the world can learn of your message and read your book.

- A number of people who read your book will not come into your building. Through your writing, however, you will still have the opportunity to influence them.

- You could either leave your current ministry field for another or leave this life for Heaven, but your ministry will continue to impact lives through the books you have written.

- You can employ your more creative side of story-telling, which most pastors use on a regular basis anyway. This method will engage people who may never pick up a non-fiction book with spiritual truths.

- If you decide to write fiction, you could reach a secular audience through your story with a subtle message of truth. Through my fiction writing, especially since my first book, I am connecting to the obvious needs people feel ("felt needs") and pointing readers to biblical principles.

I have chosen to write in such a way that attracts a secular audience. I believe this approach allows me entrance into a segment of society a preacher may never be allowed to enter. As I deal with relationship struggles in the context of adventure, romance, and suspense, I am able to contrast what happens when people choose to live life God's way.

Through social media, my website, and my blog, I can point my readers to Christ and the message of the gospel. I will hopefully gain their trust and following through my stories, and it is my prayer that readers will consider the claims of

Christ through other forms of media my book or website presents.

Can you think of additional reasons why using the hook of writing can benefit your mission?

Standing in the Gap

Multiple points of impact may be reason enough for you to begin the book you have wanted to write for much of your life. Our world needs to be impacted for Christ. Regardless of your eschatology, I think we all agree that this world as we know it will one day come to an end. We do not know how long we have to spread the message of the gospel, but it may not be long.

Can you imagine how the principles of Ezekiel 22:30 could apply to your writing ministry? Consider God's Word: *I searched for a man among them who would build up the wall and stand in the gap before Me for the land, so that I would not destroy it; but I found no one.* Will you be the one who stands in the gap?

Jesus called us to be fishers of men. If you are going to fish, you must have multiple points of impact. Writing and publishing books is a way that Christians can be encouraged, unbelievers can be reached, and the Kingdom of God can be increased for His glory.

Action Points

- Make a list of ministry hooks you use on a regular basis. Now rate them on a scale of 1-10 for their effect on accomplishing the purpose of the church.

Can you imagine adding writing to your list? How would it rate?

- I mentioned eleven advantages to writing. Review those advantages and put a star by the ones that most excite you and lead you to consider writing.

- What genre can you imagine writing? Write in the margin the type of book you would like to initially write.

- Read Ezekiel 22:30 again and ask God to help you discern whether or not writing is a good option for expanding your ministry.

Chapter Four

Half the Work is Done

Compound interest is a wonderful asset. If my mutual fund generates earnings of eight percent this year, next year those earnings are part of the principle that will earn additional income in the months to come. I love it when something I am doing today can actually accomplish more than one objective, which I connect to earning compound interest. When I cut my yard with a push lawn mower, I am cutting my yard *and* getting exercise.

As a pastor, I find that when I read for my own personal growth, it inevitably feeds my spirit with new thoughts that eventually show up in a sermon. My purpose for reading is personal growth, but the final result also includes a more informed sermon.

If you are a preacher or if you teach on a regular basis, I believe you can experience a compounding effect with your sermons or lessons. I wrote earlier in this book that if you can write a sermon, you can write a book. I would like to offer suggestions on how you can turn the sermon you plan to preach Sunday into a chapter of a book. In so doing, you are not only preaching a message, but you compound your ministry by spreading your message around the world through your writing.

Planning for Personal Growth

Before addressing your sermon, I want to write about the issue of your personal growth. As pastors or teachers, we find it is easy to focus all of our attention on sermons or lessons. We can even slip into the habit of using our quiet time only for sermon preparation.

Christians should minister out of the overflow of their personal growth. Pastors who do not have a plan for personal growth will eventually find that they are ministering from a dry, barren heart.

I have heard for years that leaders are readers. I believe Christians should be readers, and certainly, writers must be readers. Though I have never read any of Stephen King's novels, he is revered by many as a great writer. He said, "If you don't have time to read, you don't have the time (or the tools) to write."[1] You must feed your heart and your mind with books on a variety of topics.

Not only must we read, but we must also have systems to capture what we read so we can apply principles and use truths as God directs. How often have you been preparing a sermon and remembered reading something in a book that would be a perfect quote or illustration? Although the illustration would be a perfect fit, you can't remember when you read it or even what you were reading.

I have tried to develop the discipline of reading and filing daily. I began this discipline as a young pastor, and it has paid dividends in my personal growth and ministry. I love using illustrations from my files that I may have placed there five or ten years earlier. It adds depth to my preaching and writing, and it may be just the tool God uses to open up someone's heart.

In order to maximize your reading and filing, you need systems. I use a color-coded system when I read. I have a four-color pen, and I use the colors for different purposes. I use red for summary statements of a page. I can flip through a book and get the general idea by simply reading the sentences underlined in red. Green is used for illustrations. In the past, I've given a completed book to my assistant and had her type up all of the sections underlined in green so I could file the quotes and illustrations in my "illustration file." Blue is used for simply writing notes in the margin.

The next challenge is to create a useable filing system. As I am sure you know, an active file will be useful for writing sermons, books, or articles. The key is to create a system that works for *you*. I have tried a variety of techniques, including the old stand-by system of file folders in a filing cabinet organized by topic. I still use that system along with new ones.

One challenge when using illustration software is that it may not work on future computer operating system upgrades. One system I subscribe to and one that has received raving reviews is Evernote. Erick McKiddie has written an excellent blog on using Evernote that I encourage you to read.[2]

Regardless of the system you choose, remember to document your illustrations well. If I file an article from the Internet, I always copy the URL on the bottom of the article for future reference.

Which Comes First?

I have gone back and forth on this question: which comes first – the book or the sermon? I have actually done both. I wrote *Songs from the Heart: Meeting with God in the Psalms* in advance of a summer message series. I wanted my congregation to encounter God in the Psalms, but it is impossible to cover the whole book in eight Sundays of preaching. I could have spent eight years and still not covered the whole Psalter. Instead, I wrote a book to give them an additional experience in the Psalms. Granted, my book is not comprehensive, but it still enhanced my summer series. After writing and publishing my book, I expanded my ministry by selling my book on Amazon.

The advantage to writing the book first is that your congregation can use the book as a resource that will multiply the impact of your sermon. Your small groups could use the book as a study guide for discussion during the sermon series. I also think that by writing in advance of the sermon, your message will actually be more concise and better informed. The summer I preached on Psalms, I preached not only as a result of the preparation for that sermon, but also from the overflow of months of writing on the topic.

Writing the book after preaching the sermon or series is advantageous in that your preparation can be a springboard into more research for your writing. My book, *Immovable: Standing Firm in the Last Days*, is an example of this method. I preached a couple of different series, one on Bible prophecy and one on spiritual warfare, which I combined to become one book. Because it actually took me three years to complete the book, I wrote a new sermon series on the basic topics of *Immovable* and used the book as a resource for the new series.

One practice that helps in using sermon preparation for writing books is to preach a sermon series instead of just a stand-alone sermon. You may already preach in the series format, so this issue could be a moot point for you.

It is fairly easy to take a six to eight-week series and turn it into a book. Each sermon can be a chapter. Write an introduction, a conclusion, create a small group discussion guide, and you have completed your book. It is a little more complicated than that, but I think you can see the point.

In a future book of this series, I will address some legal and ethical issues you must consider. For now, just know that your church owns any intellectual property you may create for the purposes of your ministry at your church. There are some important steps for you to take so you can publish material you use in a sermon. You should also be careful about using church time to write and publish books. These challenges can be overcome, so I hope you will carefully read the material I will share at a later time.

Effective Preparation

If you are going to turn your sermon into a book, you must be thorough in your sermon preparation. I realize we should be thorough anyway, but sometimes in sermon preparation, we may take short cuts because of time constraints. For example, we can get by in sermon preparation with just writing down a quote to use as an illustration and saying, "One author said...." If you are going to use that quote in a book, it is best to go ahead and include the bibliographical information in your notes. This practice enables you to properly attribute the quote to the right author in the content of your book and to the right book in your bibliography. I appreciate authors giving me a good bibliography so I can look further into a source, if I so desire.

Not only should we make notes of our sources, but also we need to thoroughly vet our sources. I may use a source that I do not really agree with theologically or philosophically, and if it is a significant difference, it is best for me to make a statement to that effect. If I quote an author in my book or sermon, people will assume that I agree with everything that author writes. Odds are I don't. I am not saying you have to make a big deal about your differences, but you could say something like, "While (author's name) and I may differ on some issues, I really like how he addressed this subject."

Thorough preparation also means that we do not plagiarize. I once heard a speaker at a pastors' conference say, "When Chuck Swindoll preaches better sermons, so will I," and everyone laughed. We laughed because we have probably at least borrowed a thought from another pastor before. Some pastors borrow whole sermons from other pastors and preach them as if the sermon was their original work. Let's face it; that's not right.

If we use other pastors' sermons on a regular basis, it means we are not putting in the sermon preparation time needed to really hear a word from God for our own congregation. If we do use a sermon that someone else wrote, we should say so in the opening of our message.

While it may be acceptable to preach someone else's sermon occasionally if you first give them credit, it is not appropriate to include that sermon in your book. It is not just unethical, but it is actually illegal. Even if you use a quote or story or a point that someone else wrote, give them credit in your preaching and your writing.

I preached someone else's sermon one time in my ministry simply because it was so good, and my congregation needed to hear it. I told my church that I heard the particular sermon when I visited another church, and though I made some changes to it, the basic content came from another pastor.

I once heard John Maxwell tell about the pastor who said he would either be "original or nothing." Maxwell jokingly said something like, "He didn't amount to much."

Using other people's material is not wrong, as long as we give them credit. Actually, you can stand a lot taller when you're standing on someone else's shoulders. You may quote someone and then share your own original thoughts the quote stimulated.

When you use other people's material, remember that copyright laws stipulate how much of that material is accessible for your use. You may have to get written permission to include it in your book. We may quote the words from a song in a sermon, but you might be sued if you include those words in your book without first getting permission.

Even Bible editors have stipulations on how much Scripture you can quote, but they all require proper attribution regardless of the amount of text used. Various online sources are available that offer the specific laws regarding the use of Bible translations. Consider this link for an example:
http://christianity.stackexchange.com/questions/1637 7/what-major-translations-of-the-bible-are-in-the-public-domain .

Another discipline that will help turn your sermon into a book is to write out a full manuscript of your sermon. I do not always write sermon manuscripts, but I find that when I do take the time to do so, my actual preaching is better. Writing the manuscript causes me to think through not only what I am going to say, but also how I am going to say it.

I am a Bible teacher, and my teaching/preaching style feels extemporaneous. While it may feel this way, the finished product represents several steps:

- initial preparation that came in a sermon planning retreat that I take once a year;
- additional reading I may do months in advance;
- concentrated study on the overall series topic and scripture;
- around twenty hours of focused study I do in final preparation for that message;
- the filling and ministry of the Holy Spirit through me as I teach God's Word.

I find it a lot easier to translate all my work into a completed book chapter if I write out my sermon sentence-by-sentence a day or two before I deliver it. Writing a manuscript is tedious, but it pays in the long run.

I mentioned that I plan my preaching in an annual sermon retreat. When I first started going on an annual study/prayer retreat about twenty-five years ago, I received some criticism from people who felt like I was not being Spirit-led. I would always respond by saying, "Is God not powerful enough and wise enough to guide me a year in advance just as effectively as a week in advance?"

By planning my preaching, I have a better tool for developing our worship services in advance with my team. It's kind of hard to use video, interviews, drama, specific music, etc. without advance planning. I also can better plan my writing ministry. Had I not decided in August to preach through Psalms the following summer, I would not have written my book on Psalms.

I have a "Planning Your Preaching Resource" available that I am happy to share with you for free. If you will go to my website (www.timriordan.me) and click on the "Resources" tab, you will see information on how to request this short pdf document highlighting a sermon planning system I have used for years, and that system works well for me.

Offering More than Expected

An additional benefit to putting your sermon in print is that you can offer the "something extra." By something extra, I mean offering additional resources to help your reader apply the principles. With the advent of digital books, you can include links in your book to various websites.

When I preached a series on financial freedom, we included in the bulletin a link to Dave Ramsey's website where he offers various financial calculators. If I were writing a book on financial freedom, I would add the link for my readers.

If you are reading this book in digital format, you have already seen the hyperlinks included, and you may have already clicked on some of them to read the additional information. You can also create an interactive website to go along with your book, thereby expanding the experience of the reader. The options are limitless, but the impact is profound.

On July 4, 1952, Florence Chadwick was determined to become the first woman to swim the twenty-six miles that separated Catalina Island from the California coast. She had already conquered the English Channel.

Flanked by small boats to protect her from sharks, she swam for about fifteen hours before a dense fog set in. She swam for another hour before giving up because she was exhausted and could not tell how much further she had to go.

After getting into the boat and heading for shore, she discovered she had only been about one mile away from her goal when she had given up. She accomplished the feat a year later.

If you preach or teach on a regular basis, you are much more than halfway to the goal of publishing your book. Turning your sermon into a book is hard work, and at times, you may feel like giving up, but I encourage you to keep working at it. You will eventually find your ministry influence is greatly enhanced. Many more lives can be touched and changed through putting your message in print.

Action Points

- Do you have a plan for personal growth? If not, take a few moments to think about the following categories in your life:

- o   spiritual growth
- o   ministry growth
- o   relational growth
- o   physical growth
- o   financial growth.

  While you may want to decide on different broad categories, set a few goals under each growth area, and then determine some steps you will take to accomplish your goal. Include titles of books you will read, relationships you will develop, conferences you will attend, and other steps you will take to grow in that particular area.

- How many books do you read during a typical month? Do you have a system for filing illustrations and ideas you may pick up from your reading? If not, create a system that will provide useful resources for future ministry.

- Take a moment to visit the Evernote website (evernote.com) and read Eric McKiddie's blog about using Evernote as an illustration system. Would this be a good fit for you?

- Do you usually preach in series? What do you think would be some advantages to following this style of preaching? Do you have a series coming up that you think would be a good book for your congregation?

- What are some steps you should take during preparation of next week's sermon that will offer you the compounding effect of using study time for a sermon as research for a book?

- What is the "something extra" you could provide that ties into next week's sermon? Is this something you may want to include in your bulletin? How will it help your congregation take your sermon to the next level?

CHAPTER FIVE

Narrowing Your Topic

Do people ever complain about how long you preach? Sometimes I preach too long. It's just a fact. On the rare occasion that someone says something about it, I think to myself, "If you only knew what I didn't say." I find that one of the hardest things about preaching is not deciding what to say but rather deciding *what not to say*. Your writing ministry can present the same challenges.

I have spent enough time with preachers to know that previous sermons may be our favorite topic of discussion. Do I need to remind those of us who preach on a regular basis that most people really do not care about last week's sermon outline? We may think it was clever, or we may have really enjoyed focusing on a particular word we studied for about three hours. Word studies have great value, but most people do not share our passion for the exercise.

I remember hearing Rick Warren tell of a cartoon of a pastor standing behind the pulpit saying, "Interestingly enough, the Greek word for tapioca is…" Most people do not really care to know the Greek word for tapioca or whatever the word happened to have been this week.

Our preaching will obviously have its greatest impact when God's truth intersects with life's challenges. It is this intersection that provides the most important topics for writing and preaching as we seek to lead people to a passionate relationship with Jesus.

Some sermons we preach are needed for the moment, but they are not as useful for the long term. The message may have had specific application to a particular problem your church was facing, but in a few months, that problem will be a distant memory. While every message is needed (hopefully) and Spirit-led, not every sermon needs to be put into a book. How then do you narrow your writing focus?

Writing on Purpose

Consider briefly something we will study further in the next chapter. What is your purpose for writing, and what is the objective of your book? While it may be difficult to determine the objective of your book without knowing the topic, your objective may be a little more obvious than you think.

You may want to write a book that will be a devotional for your Christmas series next year. Although you may not know exactly the topic or text of your series, you may still have the objective of providing family devotionals to be used during advent. Your objective could be to offer a small group resource that will encourage community, but you may not have figured out exactly the message series that you want the book to support.

If you can decide on your broader purpose, even before determining your topic, it will greatly inform your writing. You may find that by starting your book before working on your message series, your writing process also becomes a sermon preparation tool.

You should also determine whether or not your book will be mainly for your congregation or for other believers as well. Do you want your book to be a resource for unbelievers? Do you want to focus on some aspect of discipleship or call the church to be on mission?

Think about the broad stroke of purpose, and write a page or two on what you would like to accomplish with your book. Such clarity will eventually be seen in your writing.

Writing is hard work, so you need to think of your work in this area as a stewardship. I consider reading to fall into the category of stewardship as well, though it has a variety of other purposes in our lives. I plan my reading in advance for several reasons, but one of those reasons is because I am to be a good steward of my time. I can read only so many books in a year; therefore, I must choose carefully so as not to waste my time on a book that will not accomplish God's purpose in me.

Think of writing in the same way. You can spend only so many hours writing, so do not waste your time on a manuscript that is not going to be the best option for accomplishing God's purpose.

In addition to hard work, writing takes a long time. Before you choose topics for your books, you should make sure that you are willing to spend the next twelve months or so reading and studying about that theme. I do not intend to imply that you cannot write a book in a shorter period of time, but it must be a topic about which you are willing to invest a lot of time and energy.

Consider your Preaching Plan

I find that I typically preach from series to series. Throughout my preaching calendar, I may have a Sunday set aside for a stand-alone sermon, but most of my sermons fall into a series of messages. The advantage of preaching a series is that you can use the topic to build anticipation. You can create advertising to invite people from the community. The unchurched family next door might come to a short series on Heaven or marriage if someone invites them to the first message. Stand-alone sermons are not as easily promoted.

I also believe that people think in context of themes. If I preach a series, I can build momentum leading up to the series and then from week to week within the series. This momentum factor will be compounded significantly if you also provide a companion book that you wrote.

If you plan your preaching in advance, which I highly recommend, you can look ahead at your preaching and determine which series will be the best one to use in your writing ministry. Unless I pastor a church filled with seminary students who are really into the Pentateuch, I doubt I would write a book on the laws related to the

Levitical priesthood. Look over your preaching plan and ask yourself several questions:

- Is there a particular series in my future plan that will be even better if my congregation does additional reading on the topic?
- Is there a spiritual issue I feel burdened about for my congregation or for people in general?
- Would our small groups or Sunday School classes benefit by the study of a particular topic or selection of Scripture?
- Is my congregation weak in one of the purposes of the church that could be improved through additional reading?
- Do I have a burning passion about a topic that I believe the Lord wants me to share?
- Has God shown me any new ideas or taught me any new lessons that I should share with others through writing? I find my greatest expressions in writing come from the overflow of my personal experiences with God.
- What are the felt needs of my congregation and community? While pastors and theologians may become pretty excited about topics like Kenotic theology found in Philippians 2:7, their people may be struggling with how to have family devotions or how to put life back into their marriages. They probably do not even know what *kenosis* means and do not really care.

Felt needs are the kinds of issues our people think about a lot and struggle with often. They need to hear what God says about these issues. Teaching on heavier, theological topics has its place, but the needs of your congregation will somewhat determine your sermon content.

- Is there a hot topic about which people really need to consider God's teaching? In response to the *Fifty Shades* movie that recently came out, you could have written a book about God's plan for sex in marriage. What about the issue of homosexuality and same-sex marriages? You may find it useful to write a book about living on God's truth while reflecting God's grace.

Your objective will determine your approach. Obviously, a Bible study book will be different than a book used for outreach. If your church is about to go into a building campaign, you may want to write a series of devotionals on stewardship. If I am going to try to influence unchurched people to think about spiritual things, it will be best for me to start out with a felt needs type of book. Let's not be guilty of answering questions in our writing that no one is asking.

Defining Your Brand

Your "brand" should also help you decide the topic for your book. I will focus on the issue of brand in another book in this series. For now, just know that writers are typically known for a specific theme or brand. What topic do you think about when I mention Tim

LaHaye or Joel C. Rosenberg? What comes to mind when you think of John Maxwell or Andy Stanley?

As pastors, I think we can get by with writing books that cover a broader spectrum, but your brand will help you promote your books to a certain group of people. It would have been a little odd for Dr. James Dobson to have written a book comparing Calvinism with Armenianism because his brand is the family. He built a platform on the topic of family matters, so his readers expected his books to help them with family issues.

As you look at future message series, do you have a particular series that falls in line with the issue that you most want to champion? That series may very well be the one about which you should write.

Choosing your book topic is serious work and should not be taken lightly. Your resources may influence your decision and your circumstances may offer clarity. While many issues will affect your decision, really pray through the process so as to be truly Spirit-led. We want our writing to have Kingdom impact, so we need to be tuned into what God is saying to us, so choose wisely.

Action Points
- Have you preached a sermon lately that was unique and time specific for your congregation, but would not be good to incorporate into a book?
- Think back over your preaching for the last year or two. Did you preach a series of sermons that could

have been put into a book so as to have greater impact on your congregation and people in general?

- Do you plan your preaching in advance? Make a list of advantages and disadvantages to planning your preaching six months to a year in advance. Do the advantages outweigh the disadvantages? What obstacles would you have to overcome in order to create an annual preaching calendar?
- How would planning your preaching assist you in your writing ministry?
- Do you have a sermon or series coming up in the next few months that you think would be good to put into a book?
- Have you visited my website yet to download the free resource on planning your preaching?

Chapter Six
Preparing to Write Your Book

Ancient Chinese philosopher Lao Tzu stated, "A journey of a thousand miles begins with one step."[3] For many of us, the thought of a thousand-mile journey of writing a book often keeps us from writing the first sentence.

Before I became a writer, I kept saying to myself, "If he can do it, I can do it." The "he" could have been Charles Swindoll or the pastor down the street. I would see a new book by another pastor, and it would motivate me to figure out how I could write a book as well. My problem was that I was always looking at the completed book. When I finally quit looking at the end of the journey and saw only the first step, I began my writing ministry.

Taking the First Step

What is the first step? I really think this step is more philosophical than literary. It will become for you somewhat of a guiding star, but it is an important part of the process that ultimately ends in your published book. Before you think about a topic for your book, develop an outline, or do any of the other suggestions in this chapter, you must first determine your purpose for writing.

Christian writing has a variety of purposes that are mostly valid and acceptable. Your purpose could be to write clean and entertaining books. You may be like my friend, Ron Wildes, who wrote *Swamp Ponderings*, which is a collection of entertaining stories that are sort of like modern-day parables. While one purpose is to entertain, Ron also desires to use his humorous stories to point the reader to eternal truths.

Your purpose may be to write fiction that shows the reader examples of couples who reflect biblical truths in their relationships. It could simply be to cause readers to laugh, because as the Proverb writer stated, *A joyful heart is good medicine, but a broken spirit dries up the bones* (Proverbs 17:22). My purpose for writing is to lead people to have a passionate and growing relationship with Jesus Christ.

I would urge you not to shrug off this important part of the process. This step is important, because it helps you to know what to write. Writers have many options for content, and their purpose will narrow down the genre. A clear purpose for writing is also helpful in the marketing stage, which I will cover in another book in this series.

Knowing your purpose will also provide a great tool for evaluating your writing. Writers should review their manuscripts first with their purpose clearly in mind. Purposes can be expanded. It is possible you will write additional books that actually accomplish a different purpose, but make sure that you are intentional with your writing.

While my main purpose for writing is to lead people to a passionate relationship with Jesus, I am writing this series to help pastors become writers. In a round-about way, I am still accomplishing my purpose. If you read *The Published Pastor* series and then write a book that leads people into a passionate relationship with Jesus, then my purpose will be realized.

Determining the Who? What? Why?

Once you have a good grasp on your purpose for writing, you must define the objective of your book. You should ask yourself, "Why am I writing this particular book?" Before you begin your book, write a short paragraph about what you hope to accomplish through your writing project. After the paragraph is completed, summarize it in a single sentence. Then, narrow your sentence to a simple phrase or a single word, if possible. Print this phrase or word out onto a piece of paper and keep it visible over the months you are doing research and writing your manuscript.

Writers can easily go down paths that do not accomplish their objectives and chase rabbits that are not worth the hunt. If you're not careful, a 150-page book ends up being 250 pages because your objective was not clear.

In addition to defining your objective, also define your reader. As pastors and church leaders, you may have a tendency to assume that you are writing a book every person on the planet should read. Your books will be better if you know the kind of people who will be drawn to them. It will make you hone your writing to address your audience better.

Ask yourself this question: who will read my book? Describe the person with as much detail as possible. Michael Hyatt refers to this step as a "demographic description" in his wonderful resource, *Writing a Winning Non-fiction Book Proposal.*[4] While Hyatt's book is preparing you to write a proposal for a prospective publisher, which I will explain in a chapter in the second book of this series, completing much of the exercise on the front end of writing will make your book better. This demographic description should include areas such as gender, age, education level, socioeconomic status, geographic location, theological disposition, television shows and movies they may watch, and periodicals they may read.

In addition to a demographic description, Hyatt suggests including a "psychographic description." This description points to the kinds of things that motivate your reader. By considering the motivations of your readers, you will not only know who will read your book, but also why they will read it.

By defining your objective and your audience, you might discover that one book will actually develop into two or three follow-up books. When I first wrote *Immovable: Standing Firm in the Last Days*, my objective was to equip Christians for the spiritual warfare they will experience in the last days. After concluding the main portion of the book, which dealt with the last days' implications of the spiritual armor of Ephesians 6:10-18, I really wanted to include a section on practical application. This realization led me to write a parenting chapter on preparing our children to stand firm. The only problem is that when I began working with a publisher, one of the editors told me that my book was too long. I eventually cut the last two chapters, and I set them aside for follow-up books.

Because of the demographics and psychographics of my book, I am now putting material together for my next *Immovable* book called *Immovable Kids*. I suppose I will write a third book called *Immovable Churches*.

Finding Your Creative Zone

Everyone is different, so the next step should be expressed in writers' lives according their personal tastes and temperaments. You will find it useful to discover an environment that will promote creativity and efficiency.

I must admit that I write in a variety of places, so I do not always follow my own advice; however, the proper environment helps you to be effective.

I have an office in the administrative area of my church that is filled with all manner of resources for church leadership, discipleship, ministry, and sermon preparation. I am currently creating a study in our building that I will use simply for sermon preparation. I will store only resources used for message preparation in my new study. I will use this new area for creating materials that lead people to have a passionate relationship with Jesus. These materials will obviously show up in the form of sermons, but this environment will also support my writing ministry.

Though the study is not complete, I already use it for studying at times. When I walk into this environment, I want either to pray, study, or write. I will never use this area for administration, counseling, or meetings.

I have a place I jokingly refer to as my office annex. I actually have two different places like that. One of them is the McDonald's down the street, and the other is Wendy's. I enjoy going to these places to get away from my office to think and write. As a matter of fact, I wrote part of this book while drinking coffee at McDonald's. This environment is not nearly as inspiring as an office with a plate glass window overlooking the Appalachian Mountains, but for now, it will work. The coffee is good and inexpensive, and I get free refills.

Everyone's creative zone is going to be different, and mine fluctuates. The point is this: *find yours.*

If you can create your writing space in a home office, I suggest you have a marker board or bulletin board upon which you can place visuals that will help you formulate ideas. Have sticky notes handy along with paper clips.

I like having a shelf on my desk where I keep resources used strictly for my current writing project. I do not keep a dictionary or thesaurus on my shelf, because I use my computer for that purpose, but I do have a copy of *The Chicago Manual of Style* nearby. Along with those particular resources, you should consider keeping other materials that help you in writing.

Creating a Writing Calendar

The next step in the writing process is to create a writing calendar. I preface these comments by reminding you to remain flexible and know that you are not always in charge of your calendar. For example, an editor may take six months to complete the editing on your book instead of the two months you had desired.

With flexibility at the forefront of your mind, decide when you would like to complete your book. Calendaring is not always an easy task, and your preaching plan may determine your deadlines. If you plan to use your book as a companion for a summer series, as I did with my book on Psalms, then you need to complete everything so as to have your books in hand by the third Sunday of May.

For my Psalms project, I set a deadline for completion on May 1. Because I self-published my book, I knew that I would upload my finished product and have the proof copy within a week. Once I approved the copy, it took approximately two weeks to receive my first order. I knew this schedule was cutting it close, so I took steps to move it along. The May 1st deadline drove much of the other plans I added to my calendar.

I do not suggest you rush your project, as I was forced to do. My story does show, however, that you can write a 256-page book in four months.

I worked backward from May 1st and determined how many chapters I needed to write in a week. I gave myself a week to finalize the formatting and to complete the last-minute tasks needed before sending it off to be printed. Because I was quite rushed on the project, I needed to have my book edited as I wrote it, so my editor had to be willing to follow this plan. On a calendar, I wrote out my plans to write chapters on thirty different Psalms along with a few chapters of introduction to the book of Psalms.

Toward the end, I had nights where I did not get much sleep. But with God's help, I finished the project on time. I added dates to my calendar to work with my graphic artist for the cover design along with time to create the final interior look for publishing (remember that I self-published).

I received my first big shipment of books before the last Sunday of May so my congregation could purchase copies to go along with the summer series that started on the following Sunday. It was a little too close for comfort, but God is continuing to use this book in the lives of readers in places I never imagined.

The first part of your writing calendar will include a season of research. I find that while I am constantly doing research throughout my writing project, a period devoted to good and well-documented research on the front end will save many hours later. Do not take shortcuts on this phase of writing. You do not want your book to be a repeat of another author. You want to write something that will represent thorough study, careful thought, and regular prayer.

Although your greatest research assistant may be Google, create a bibliography of books you plan to purchase or at least borrow for your project. Begin by finding other books on your topic. After reading them, determine how your book will deal with the topic in a fresh way or how it will address issues not covered in the other books. You could even reference these books in your own writing.

Before writing this book, I read Josh Hunt's *The Pastor's Guide to Book Publishing*. It is a short book, but it offers some great insight and good ideas. It was the only book on writing specifically for pastors that I was able to find.

Your research will probably include more resources than just books. You could attend a conference that is related to your topic or listen to a few related podcasts. Your research may include interviewing people who are experts in a field related to your topic.

I wrote earlier that I have written fiction for fun, but it has turned into a ministry that I did not at first anticipate. A few months after releasing my first novel, I began receiving e-mails through my publishing website (www.greentreepublishers.com) asking when the sequel was coming out. I had not planned a sequel, but I realized that I could reach a totally different audience through a fictional story.

My first work of fiction was not as well-thought-out, and I didn't really consider possible spiritual themes, other than wholesome characters with integrity and solid morals. In my sequel (which is now book 3 of the series), I developed a plot that promotes marriage and healthy relationships and offers secular readers a gentle nudge toward the difference Christ can make in their lives.

Much of the action of my second novel takes place on the island of Eleuthera, in the Bahamas, so I contacted a few people on the island and built an online relationship with them. They provided me with enough detail and confirmation so that the description of island life was accurate. Whom should you contact so that your book will be better or more thoroughly researched?

At this point in the writing process, you may not have written the first word in your manuscript, but you have laid a solid foundation that will take you miles down the road toward a completed project. If you get bogged down or even take shortcuts in these steps, you might get overwhelmed and never complete your book. Keep your goal in mind and tackle these first steps with the knowledge that they are moving you toward the second stage of book writing.

Action Points

- Have you allowed the challenges of writing a book to keep you from accomplishing your writing objectives? What decisions do you need to make so that accomplishing your writing goals can be met?

- What is your purpose for writing? Take some time to work through this step and write out a purpose statement.

- Have you already considered a book topic? What will your objective be? If you have not considered a topic yet, pick a series you will preach in the future and imagine writing a book to accompany it. Write out an objective statement as if you plan to write a companion book for the series.

- Where is your optimum writing place? How can you create an environment that will encourage creativity?

- Pick a sermon series topic that you think would make a good book. Create a possible calendar you could follow. I encourage you to pray through this process. God may possibly lead you to a topic that ends up being your first book. Divide your project into times for research, writing, editing, formatting, and interior and exterior work.

- Make a list of people you should contact to better prepare to write your book. What will you do to connect with these people?

- Have you downloaded Book Two in the *Published Pastor* series? It will be available in mid-June, 2015. If you have not picked it up yet, visit Amazon and get ready for the second phase of writing and publishing books.

FINAL THOUGHTS...

I am assuming by now that you are chomping at the bit to put pen to paper. You may have already begun writing the rough draft of your manuscript. I hope that through the pages of this first book in *The Published Pastor* series you have been both challenged and encouraged.

This first book has provided you important foundational information to help you get started with your writing ministry. I have also connected you with various resources that will help you along the way. My initial goal has been to help you consider the possibilities of writing your first book. I am hoping that you have made a commitment to take the first steps toward being a published author.

The second book in the series is entitled *How to Write and Publish a Book*. It will help you accomplish the following objectives:

- Complete the writing phase of your book.
- Finalize your manuscript for publication.
- Compare self-publishing to traditional publishing.

- Help you to know what to do to turn your completed manuscript into a self-published book.
- Guide you through the process of designing the interior and exterior of your book.

I spent many hours mastering the art and science of self-publishing. I will pass along this critical information to you through the second book in this series.

The third book is entitled *Reaching a Broader Audience through Marketing*. Marketing might be the furthest consideration from your mind right now, but I do suggest you read the third book before you publish your manuscript. The information you will glean from book two will need to be reviewed in detail as you prepare your book for publishing. You will discover that some of the steps described in book three should be taken even before completing your manuscript.

The final book of the series will address some of the legal and ethical issues you will face as an author. I will share critical information with you that must not be avoided. If you are not aware of these matters and if you do not take precautionary steps, you could face serious consequences.

The writing and publishing journey is an exciting one. You will have the opportunity to impact people in such a way you never dreamed possible. I would love to have the opportunity to pray for you and to offer my personal help and encouragement. I invite you to join the writers' group on Facebook and contact me by e-mail (triordan8@gmail.com). Let me know what you are working on and how I can help you.

May God bless you and your ministry as you expand your opportunities for Kingdom influence! God will be honored as you bear much fruit.

Note from the Author

I am honored that you have made the investment of time and money to read this first book of my *Published Pastor* series. I hope it has been helpful, and I trust you are encouraged to take the next step in writing your book. I mentioned in the book that I am happy to help you any way I can, and I did not make this offer lightly. Please feel free to contact me, even if you just have a question about your own project. I would also love to have the privilege to pray for you as you undertake your own writing project.

At times, I have needed a question answered by someone with experience. You will face the same challenge, so I offer myself to serve you any way needed. I will put my contact information below.

Will you consider doing me the honor of writing a brief review on Amazon.com? That would be most helpful for me. If you are interested in having me come speak at your church or to your pastor's group, I will do my best to make myself available to serve you. I have led conferences on writing and publishing as well as spoken on various topics including that of my book: *Immovable: Standing Firm in the Last Days*.

It is my prayer that God will use you and your ministry greatly in the days to come. May He bear eternal fruit through your faithful service.

Tim Riordan
May 31, 2015

You can follow me or contact me through the Internet and social media outlets listed below:

Personal Website and Blog:
http://www.timriordan.me

Facebook Author Page: http://on.fb.me/1CUNWRm

Facebook Pastors' Writers Group:
http://on.fb.me/1Pw2QsU

Twitter: https://twitter.com/tim_riordan

Goodreads: http://bit.ly/1HrAicJ

E-mail: triordan8@gmail.com

Books from Greentree Publishers

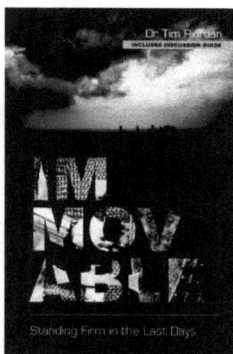

Immovable: Standing Firm in the Last Days

By Tim Riordan

Does Bible prophecy indicate that we are living in the last days? What should Christians do to be ready for the days ahead? Dr. Tim Riordan shares biblical truths on Bible prophecy and how the Church can stand firm in the last days. Through a careful study of Bible prophecy related to the last days, Dr. Riordan shows the connection between the spiritual armor of Ephesians 6 and the spiritual warfare that will take place in the days leading up to Christ's return. This book also offers a small group discussion guide. You can find more information about this book on Dr. Tim Riordan's website at www.timriordan.me. Available in paperback and e-book formats from your favorite retailer.

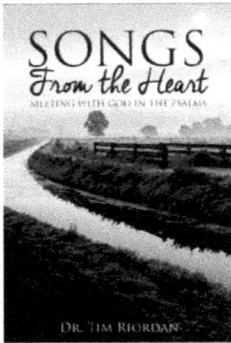

Songs from the Heart:
Meeting with God in the Psalms
By Tim Riordan

Songs from the Heart: Meeting with God in the Psalms is a Bible study/devotional on one of the most loved books of the Bible: Psalms. Join Dr. Tim Riordan as he shares insights on these beloved passages through Bible teaching and storytelling, making personal application to your life. This book is available in paperback and e-book formats from your favorite retailer.

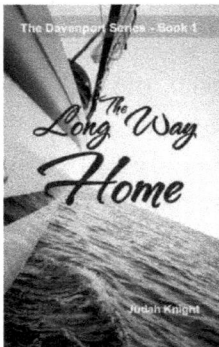

The Long Way Home
By Judah Knight

Dive into an adventure of scuba diving, treasure hunting, danger and suspense in Judah Knight's exciting novel, The Long Way Home. When Meg was stranded in the Caribbean, her life was dramatically changed through an encounter with an old friend that turned into adventure, danger, discovery, and love. Enjoy Judah Knight's flinch-free fiction that is safe for the whole family. Available in paperback and e-book formats from your favorite retailer.

Consider other books in the Davenport Series

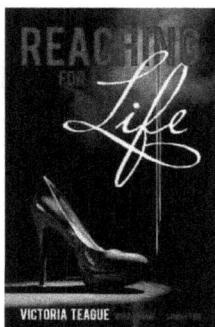

The Davenport Series Book 2

Hope for Tomorrow

Judah Knight

The Davenport Series Book 3

Finding My Way

Judah Knight

Davenport Series - Prequel

A Girl Can Always **HOPE**

Judah Knight

Reaching for Life
By Victoria Teague with Connie J. Singleton

Following an eleven-year cocaine addiction and a dangerous career as a dancer in Atlanta's sex industry, Victoria Teague experienced what can only be called a miraculous rescue. For ten years after she left the clubs, she sat respectably in the pews of her church with a grateful heart and a zip-locked mouth. She built an entirely new life on top of embarrassing secrets from her past, and only a precious, trusted few knew her spiritual rags-to-riches story. That is until one ordinary day when she was asked to do anything *but* the ordinary. On that day, she was called not only to share her secrets, but also to spotlight them. To use them as her "street cred" to minister to other women in the strip clubs who desperately need a lifeline like the one she was offered. To seek the lost and give them hope for a better life. Available in paperback and e-book formats from your favorite retailer.

Notes

[1] Stephen King, *On Writing: The Memoir of the Craft* (New York, Scribner), 2000, *On Writing* 1.

[2] Evernote is an iCloud based note taking system that allows you to store about anything as a "note", and it offers options of creating searchable topics for any note you store. This feature makes Evernote perfect for a sermon illustration file. Because it is an iCloud based program, you can update your files on a computer and the update immediately shows up on any of your Internet devices. To read the blog, visit the following site:
http://www.pastoralized.com/2011/11/09/build-an-illustration-file-thats-easy-to-use-with-evernote.

[3] Originally, this quote came from Chapter 64 of a Chinese Classic Text called *Tao Te Ching*. Though authorship has been debated, this quote is often attributed to Chinese philosopher Lao Tzu.

[4] https://michaelhyatt.com/writing-a-winning-book-proposal